TERRORIST
DOSSIERS

RAGING WITHIN

Ideological TERRORISM

Samuel M. KATZ

Lerner Publications Company/Minneapolis

Publishers Note: The information in this book was current at the time of publication. However, the publisher is aware that news involving current events dates quickly. Please refer to the websites on pages 68–69 for places to go to obtain up-to-date information.

Lerner Publications Company
A division of Lerner Publishing Group
241 First Avenue North
Minneapolis, Minnesota U.S.A.

Website address: www.lernerbooks.com

Library of Congress Cataloging-in-Publication Data

Katz, Samuel M., 1963–
     Raging within: ideological terrorism / by Samuel M. Katz.
          p.   cm. — (Terrorist dossiers)
     Summary: Examines 20th century political violence in Europe, Asia, and South America, including the Red Army Faction, 17 November, and Túpac Amaru.
     Includes bibliographical references and index.
     ISBN: 0–8225–4032–0 (lib. bdg. : alk. paper)
     1. Terrorism—Juvenile literature. 2. Political violence—Juvenile literature. [1. Terrorism. 2. Political violence.] I. Title. II. Series.
     HV6431.K318 2004
     303.6'25'0904—dc21   2003002311

Manufactured in the United States of America
1 2 3 4 5 6 – DP – 09 08 07 06 05 04

CONTENTS

anti-Western: any group or philosophy opposed to the capitalist democratic governments of Europe and the United States

capitalism: an economic system in which private individuals or groups own businesses and competition is encouraged. The system involves a free market in which buyers and sellers, rather than the government, control trade by determining prices, production, and distribution. Most modern Western-style democratic nations, such as the United States and Great Britain, have mixed capitalist economies in which the government controls some aspects of business and trade.

Cold War: the term for hostilities between Western-style democracies, such as the United States and Great Britain, and the Soviet Union and its allies following World War II (1939-1945)

Communism: a social and political philosophy that urges the overthrow of the capitalist system in a workers' revolution. In place of capitalism, Communism establishes a system in which property is owned by the whole community rather than by individuals. The community also controls the means for producing and distributing goods (such as farm crops or steel).

left wing: a general political policy based on reforming the established political system on behalf of working-class people. Left-wing thinkers are also called leftists.

Karl Marx: a nineteenth-century German philosopher and writer. His works *The Communist Manifesto* and *Das Kapital* form the basis of Marxism.

Marxism: an economic and social system based on the writings of Karl Marx. In Marxism, the reforms of socialism are only a step toward establishing a Communist state.

North Atlantic Treaty Organization (NATO): a defensive alliance between the United States and other democratic nations. Established in 1949, NATO was set up to protect Western Europe against Soviet aggression during the Cold War.

radicalism: any political theory or movement that advocates extreme change from the existing government or political system

right wing: a general political policy usually strongly opposed to social and economic change in favor of traditional practices

socialism: a political movement that supports governmental control and ownership of major industries, trade, banking, and public utilities. Most socialists believe in reforming a country's existing system through peaceful and democratic action.

Vladimir Ilich Lenin: a Russian Marxist who led the 1917 Russian Revolution and established the Union of Soviet Socialist Republics (USSR)

World War II: from 1939 to 1945, a military conflict that pitted the Allies (including Great Britain, France, the USSR, and the United States) against the Axis (Germany, Italy, and Japan)

INTRODUCTION

On the morning of June 8, 2000, Brigadier Stephen Saunders was commuting to work through the northern suburbs of Athens, Greece. A military expert, Saunders was assigned to the British embassy in the Greek capital. As he sat stuck in heavy traffic, two men on a motorbike pulled up next to Saunders's car. One took a .45-caliber pistol from his leather jacket, raised it at the car window, and began firing. Alone and unarmed, Saunders could do nothing to protect himself from the sudden attack. He was struck by bullets in the hands and stomach. The terrorists sped away. Saunders died later in an Athens hospital.

Twelve years earlier and several hundred miles away in the Italian port city of Naples, a powerful car bomb exploded outside a social club for American soldiers. The bomber, Junzo Okudaira, hoped to kill as many people as possible. Armed with automatic weapons and grenades, Okudaira was also prepared to fight to the death with anyone who tried to stop him. The blast killed five people and wounded dozens more.

These two terrorist attacks, though committed in different countries more than a decade apart, had a frightening similarity. The men who killed Brigadier Saunders and the man who planted the car bomb both belonged to organizations whose ideologies—political beliefs—pushed them toward a course of action outside the normal political system. Beyond voting, beyond organizing protests, beyond publishing antigovernment literature, these terrorist organizations believed that violent means were justified to achieve their political goals.

Many of these ideologies have their roots in the violence and destruction of World War II (1939–1945). The war had left Europe and parts of Asia in ruins. Reconstruction magnified the power of the United States, which spearheaded the recovery in Western Europe and Japan, and of the Soviet Union, which brought its Communist ideology to Eastern Europe. Their resulting intense rivalry, called the Cold War, would have a far-reaching impact throughout the world.

Less than two decades after the war, the economies of many of the former combatants were booming. But many students saw their governments and their country's middle class as complacent and idle. While the middle class spent money on large homes and expensive cars, lower-class workers struggled to pay rent and feed their families. These frustrations festered and led to student protests, which spawned many radical political organizations in the 1960s.

One such radical system—Marxist socialism, named after its creator, Karl Marx—called for everyone to have a more equal share in a country's wealth. In Marxism, socialism was a step toward Communism, under which the whole community would own and operate farms and factories. But according to Marxism, before a Communist state could be established, the workers had to overthrow the country's current government, seizing power and property from the middle and upper classes. For Marx, the civil conflicts he saw "raging within existing society" were just a precursor of the class warfare to come. It was up to Marxist revolutionaries, many of whom had taken up terrorist causes as students, to stage the warfare in their own

A soldier runs through a ruined street in France in 1944.

countries and to back class warfare throughout the world.

Operating from the cities of Europe to the jungles of South America, terrorist groups took up revolutionary ideologies such as Marxism. Whether they have given up their battles or are still a violent threat, their stories comprise the history of ideologically inspired terrorist movements in the twentieth century.

Andreas Baader: a West German student activist and one of the founders of the Red Army Faction

East Germany: a European country established as a Communist state by Soviet forces in 1949 after Germany's defeat in World War II. After the Soviet Union collapsed in 1990, East Germany was reunited with West Germany as the Federal Republic of Germany (or simply Germany).

Gudrun Ensslin: a West German student activist who is often considered the brains behind the Red Army Faction

Red Army Faction (RAF): a West German terrorist group most active in the late 1960s and 1970s. The RAF was inspired by Marxist politics and anti-American sentiment. The popular name of the group, the Baader-Meinhof Gang, comes from its founders.

Ulrike Meinhof: a West German radical journalist and one of the founders of the Red Army Faction

USSR: the Union of Soviet Socialist Republics. Commonly called the Soviet Union, the USSR was founded as a Communist state in 1922 after the Russian Revolution. The USSR consisted of fifteen republics spanning from Eastern Europe across northern Asia. The Soviet Union collapsed in 1990.

West Germany: a European country established as a democracy in 1949 after Germany's defeat in World War II. It was reunited with East Germany in 1990 as the Federal Republic of Germany (or simply Germany).

GERMANY:
THE RED ARMY FACTION
(RAF)

Eager to shed its Nazi history, West Germany was reborn after World War II as a model state of prosperity and tolerance. It was one of the most liberal countries in Europe. But West Germany sat on the front line of the Cold War, caught in the intense hostility between the Soviet Union and the United States. Just across the Berlin Wall, a police-patrolled concrete divider, was East Germany, a Soviet Communist state. West Germany was a constant target of East German spies looking to disrupt its economy, its government, and even its college campuses.

German leader Adolf Hitler gives a Nazi salute during a military rally. The Nazi regime and the Holocaust were a bitter legacy for Germany's postwar generation.

GERMANY AND THE BERLIN WALL

In 1945 World War II allies Great Britain, France, the United States, and the Soviet Union divided Germany into four sections. Three sections formed West Germany. The fourth section, controlled by the Soviets, became East Germany. Berlin, Germany's former capital, was divided in half. Great Britain, France, and the United States controlled West Berlin. East Berlin was controlled by the Soviets.

Over the next several years, the Cold War produced a bitter rivalry between the Soviet Union and its former allies. Although East Germany was a fairly successful Communist state, many East Germans believed the chance for a better life lay in West Germany. After thousands of East Germans fled, the East German government began closing the border. By 1952 the only way out was through West Berlin.

This did not stop East German flight. More than one million East Germans left through West Berlin between 1952 and 1961. The East German government grew desperate. On August 13, 1961, East German soldiers were sent out in the middle of the night to erect barbed-wire fences between East and West Berlin. Within two days, the fences were replaced in sections with a twelve-foot-high concrete wall. Eventually the Berlin Wall spread 100 miles along the border between East and West Germany. The only openings were heavily guarded border crossings called checkpoints. Escape became a deadly risk. At least 170 people died or were killed by East German guards while trying to cross the border.

The Berlin Wall stood for twenty-eight years. By the fall of 1989, the East German government was on the verge of collapse. Germans from both sides took up sledgehammers and began demolishing the wall. ■

A man walks along the Berlin Wall in 1962.

West Germany also became a strategic base for anti-Soviet military and spying operations.

Many of the West Germans drawn to Communist or socialist ideologies were well educated and middle class. Born at the end of World War II, this generation was too young to remember the horrors of the Nazi regime, and to their elders, they did not seem to appreciate the freedom and opportunities of postwar West Germany. Later scholars have also suggested that West German student protesters felt a tremendous guilt for their country's Nazi past. By rebelling against the German establishment, they could voice their opposition to the institutions that had allowed the Nazis to come to power.

BAADER-MEINHOF'S BEGINNINGS | One of the
most violent student groups was West Germany's Red Army Faction (RAF). The RAF subscribed to Marx's class warfare ideas. It believed that violence was necessary to overthrow West Germany's social and economic class structure. The RAF wanted to replace the capitalist democracy with a Marxist socialist state. The organization was popularly called the Baader-Meinhof Gang after Andreas Baader and Ulrike

Communist students demonstrate in Paris in 1968. Political demonstrations across Europe in the 1960s inspired more radical action from groups like the Red Army Faction.

Meinhof, two West German radical activists who fit the profile of educated Communists turned violent.

Andreas Baader was a one-time juvenile delinquent, reportedly intelligent but aimless. His girlfriend, Gudrun Ensslin, introduced him to radical politics. Ulrike Meinhof was a respected journalist raised in a socialist family. Although her name became a symbol of radical violence, Meinhof actually had little to do with the day-to-day affairs of the gang. Baader, the true terrorist leader, ran the group along with Ensslin, the true revolutionary.

The leaders of the RAF were, in their own way, charismatic and appealing. The group's revolutionary zeal attracted followers throughout West Germany and in neighboring countries such as Austria and France. Baader, Meinhof, and Ensslin built an extensive network of hard-core sympathizers who shared their disgust with modern West

Andreas Baader is shown in a 1972 photograph. For some, Baader's good looks and macho swagger made him a romantic revolutionary figure.

German society. The RAF organized itself into an underground army of commanders, operational officers, bomb builders, and assassins. The group claimed it followed a political philosophy of liberal Communism, but its demands for political reform were often vague. The violence of revolution seemed more important to the RAF than the peaceful Marxist state it was supposed to produce.

In their first notable action, in 1968, Baader, Ensslin, and a few followers set fire to a Frankfurt department store, striking at what they saw as a symbol of capitalism. They were arrested but escaped on bail. Only Baader was rearrested. After two years in prison, Baader escaped from police custody with Meinhof's help. The group spent the next two years robbing banks, issuing statements to the press, and collecting weapons. They became well-known figures in West Germany.

Then in May 1972, the gang launched an intense two-week terrorist campaign. They bombed the U.S. Army headquarters in Frankfurt and two German police headquarters. They wired the car of a

West German judge with explosives, leaving the judge's wife permanently crippled. They set off several bombs in the offices of a West German newspaper, severely injuring seventeen employees. They bombed another U.S. Army base in Heidelberg, killing three young soldiers and wounding several others. The bloody campaign shocked the West German public, and the police intensified their search for the radicals.

Baader, Meinhof, Ensslin, and other gang members were captured in June 1972. After the longest and most expensive trial in German history, they were convicted of murder and terrorism. After the founders' imprisonment, the RAF's second tier of leadership voiced its determination to shake West Germany out of its sense of security.

Throughout the 1970s, many viewed the RAF as Europe's most deadly urban terrorist group, even though its true rank-and-file never numbered more than fifty people. The RAF operated in small cells (subgroups), each with its own commander. One cell never knew about the activities of other cells or the identities of other operatives. The true lifeline for this small underground army was a much larger base of intellectuals and sympathizers who provided money, places to live, and transportation.

THE MIDDLE EAST CONNECTION

The Marxist call for a global revolution put the RAF in league with Palestinian terrorists working to oust the State of Israel from the Middle East. Palestinian training camps in Lebanon were ramshackle universities for the study of guerrilla warfare—ideal places for the German terrorists to plan and train. In return, the Palestinians received the RAF's help in buying weapons and ammunition. The RAF also provided a pool of non-Arab personnel that could be used for attacks against Israeli targets. Where an Arab might attract the suspicion of Israeli guards or soldiers, a white European would not. ■

| THE GERMAN AUTUMN | The RAF had always targeted U.S. and North Atlantic Treaty Organization (NATO) military bases in West Germany. But in the next phase of operations, the RAF decided to strike at financial targets, such as millionaire business leaders, hoping to cause grave insecurity at the very top of West German society.

On September 6, 1977, the group kidnapped Hanns-Martin Schleyer, the president of a powerful business association and an executive with a large German auto company. The kidnapping set off a series of events that came to be known by the somber title, "the German Autumn."

■ ■

A Textbook Attack

West German authorities had realized *that the RAF was targeting symbols of West German capitalism, and they offered Hanns-Martin Schleyer police protection. It didn't help. The RAF's ambush of Schleyer's car was lightning fast and precise. On a busy street in the West German city of Cologne, an RAF team stopped Schleyer's Mercedes. They surrounded the car and peppered it with bursts of machine-gun fire. The three police officers protecting Schleyer were gunned down. Schleyer's chauffeur was also executed. Schleyer was taken hostage.*

The next day, the kidnappers released a photo of Schleyer, obviously beaten and holding up

Hanns-Martin Schleyer appears in an RAF ransom demand holding up a dated poster. The picture was released to prove that Schleyer was still alive.

an RAF poster. The RAF demanded a large ransom for Schleyer's safe return. They also demanded the release of several RAF leaders in jail in West Germany. The RAF prisoners were to be released and allowed to fly to any country they chose. Negotiations would go on for weeks.

■ ■

To the West German police, Schleyer's kidnapping showed how dangerous the RAF had become. Lawmakers agreed. The government passed emergency regulations unheard of in liberal postwar West Germany. The regulations prohibited all contact with and between terrorists in prison. The RAF could not pass information to each other and, through attorneys and visitors, to operatives throughout Europe. Authorities also began the largest wiretapping operation in law enforcement history, listening in on much of West Germany's telephone traffic.

Negotiations for Schleyer's release and the RAF prisoners stumbled on. After weeks the RAF began a desperate operation. On October 13, 1977, a team of Palestinian and RAF operatives hijacked a German Lufthansa airplane shortly after takeoff. Most of the hostages on board were West German tourists. The terrorists demanded that the West German government release RAF prisoners in exchange for the hostages.

For days the hijacked aircraft bounced around the Mediterranean and the Middle East. And the hijackers continued to demand the release of their comrades. At the port city of Aden, Yemen, the hijackers executed the plane's captain and dumped his body onto the tarmac. The plane then took off for Mogadishu, Somalia.

On the night of October 17, 1977, specially trained West German counterterrorist commandos landed secretly at the Mogadishu airport. They stormed the hijacked plane, killed three of the four hijackers, and rescued the hostages. Back in their West German prison cells, the RAF leadership heard of the success of the counterterrorist raid. The next morning, many of them, including Andreas Baader and Gudrun Ensslin, committed suicide. Some used guns their lawyers had smuggled into the prison. Some hung themselves in their cells.

On October 19, Hanns-Martin Schleyer's body was discovered in the trunk of a car in France. He had been shot in the back of the head to avenge the Mogadishu raid and the RAF suicides.

Even in a decade full of bloody terrorist attacks, ordinary West Germans were shocked by Schleyer's kidnapping and murder. They saw these acts as cold blooded and senseless. It also seemed to indicate the beginning of real class warfare inside West Germany—the elimination of the rich and ruling classes.

The West German government responded harshly. Politicians allowed the country's intelligence and police agencies broad powers to investigate and prosecute the remaining RAF leadership. Security forces dedicated enormous resources to countering the RAF.

Wanted posters of RAF operatives were hung in every West German train station, post office, library, and university. The government offered rewards for any information leading to the arrest of the RAF hierarchy. Treating the RAF threat like a war, teams of heavily armed

Millions of RAF wanted posters were distributed across West Germany in the 1970s. Under rows of jarring black and white mugshots, the posters urged any citizen with information about the RAF to phone the police.

police raided terrorist hideouts throughout the country, as did intelligence agents in neighboring countries. These efforts resulted in the arrests of many RAF leaders and supporters. But no matter how hard it tried, German law enforcement could not entirely crush the group's revolutionary spirit. The overthrow of the West German government remained the organization's objective throughout the 1980s.

THE FINAL DAYS OF THE RAF

In the end, the failure of an ideology accomplished what the West German police could not. The 1990 collapse of the Soviet regime in the USSR disillusioned many inside the RAF and many of its Communist supporters. The failure of Communism also ended Germany's division. East and West Germany were officially reunified on October 3, 1990. In the face of these democratic triumphs, the RAF's Communist ideology seemed outdated. Many RAF sympathizers simply disappeared from the radar screen. Others still preached revolution while easing themselves back into German society, middle aged and middle class—the very people the RAF had once targeted.

There were a few last gasps. In 1991 the group took credit for the assassination of a government official overseeing the reform of East German businesses. Also in 1991, during the Persian Gulf War, the RAF attacked the U.S. embassy in Bonn with machine guns and grenades. But unlike previous RAF attacks, the assault was amateurish and caused little damage.

The RAF was dealt a further blow in 1994, when German counterterrorist police ambushed and killed Wolfgang Grams, an RAF commander. Although the RAF wanted to portray Grams's death as a cold-blooded police execution, they were unable to make political use of it. The German public was not interested in rekindling the bloody days of the 1970s.

In 1997 German authorities announced that they no longer considered the RAF a serious terrorist threat. Most of its leaders were dead or in jail, while many of the group's one-time sympathizers had become disillusioned with its brutality. In April 1998, in a letter faxed to the Reuters news agency, the RAF announced it was disbanding.

COMMUNISM AND THE COLOR RED

Red was a traditional color in Russia for generations. After the Russian Revolution in 1917, Lenin adopted red as the color for the flag of the new USSR. To the bright red background he added a yellow hammer (symbol of the factory worker) and sickle (symbol of the farm worker). From 1918, the army of the Soviet Union was called the Red Army.

Many modern Communist groups, including the Red Army Faction, have used red to express solidarity with Soviet political ideas. The groups often include red in their names or use the color in their flags or emblems. To the modern Communist, red is the color of revolution. ∎

A Soviet military parade carries a red banner with images of *(left to right)* Karl Marx, Friedrich Engels, and Vladimir Lenin.

Aldo Moro: an Italian politician kidnapped and murdered by the Red Brigades in 1978

anti-imperialism: the rejection of one country's efforts to colonize or take political power in another country

fascism: a political movement that demands absolute loyalty to a nation or race. Fascist governments are usually led by a dictator and include violent repression of any opposition.

Italian Socialist Party: a political organization founded in Italy in the nineteenth century. Socialists believe in change through political processes and the protection of working-class people.

Red Brigades: a Marxist terrorist organization active in Italy in the 1970s and 1980s. The Red Brigades wanted a revolution in which Italy's capitalist system would be replaced by a Communist government.

Renato Curcio: the founder of the Red Brigades. Born in 1941, he became interested in radical politics as a student at an Italian university. Arrested in 1976, he remains in prison in Italy.

ITALY:
THE RED BRIGADES

The violence of the Red Army Faction reflected a generation's extreme dissatisfaction with the materialistic democracy of postwar West Germany. In Italy, around the same time, the mood of discontent and revolution was just as strong among the upper-class children of the postwar generation.

Yet Communism had had a long history in Italian politics, beginning in the late nineteenth century. The country's Socialist Party hoped to take advantage of a series of labor strikes in the early 1900s to gain control of the factories. But the Socialists were not unified, and arguing among themselves often eroded whatever political gains were reached. A Socialist named Benito Mussolini, cast out of the party for his violent tactics, seized power in 1922. His new Fascist Party took control of the Italian government and remained in power for more than twenty years. Mussolini later aligned himself with Nazi Germany during World War II.

Benito Mussolini *(center left)*, Adolf Hitler *(center right)*, and their ministers emerge from a meeting in Munich, Germany, in 1938.

Communism remained secretly popular inside Italy during the Mussolini years, kept alive by intellectuals and activists. In 1946, after Mussolini's death and the end of the war, Italy became a democratic republic. But the Italian economy was in chaos. The war had ruined factories, railroads, villages, and farms. Food shortages neared famine levels. Moderate political parties seemed unable to solve these postwar problems. More people began turning to the Communist and Socialist Parties.

Italian university students were also frustrated by the instability of the Italian parliament. New governments had been voted in and out of office almost every year since the war had ended. Parliament seemed hopelessly ineffective. As a result, support for the Communist Party grew especially strong on the campuses of the country's numerous universities.

| THE RED BRIGADES STEP IN | As years passed with

no great political reforms, student frustration found violent expression in the Red Brigades (Brigate Rosse in Italian). Former Italian student activists founded the Red Brigades in 1969. Like other hard-core Marxist-Leninists, the group was anti-Western and wanted to replace the Italian government with a Communist state. The Red Brigades saw itself as the advance guard of this revolution, working among the lower classes to set the stage for class warfare.

The Red Brigades' vision had the support of Italy's radical intellectuals, many of whom were university professors. Violent tactics did not trouble most radicals, who thought assassinations and bombings were necessary tools in the movement's attempts to bring down a capitalist economy. The Red Brigades' leadership came from all parts of Italian society—Catholic school students, university students, trade unionists, and leaders of Communist youth movements.

Renato Curcio was one of the founders and most important first-generation leaders of the Red Brigades. Curcio had a poor and troubled childhood, but he was an excellent student and won a scholarship to the University of Trento in northern Italy. There he became immersed in modern philosophy and began his drift toward the radical left. By the late 1960s, he had committed himself to a violent Marxist revolution. In 1969 Curcio married Mara Cagol, a fellow radical. After being arrested for a protest takeover of a vacant house, the couple went completely underground and became hard-core terrorists.

From 1972 to 1975, they led the Red Brigades on a lethal campaign of bombings, assassinations, and kidnappings.

The Red Brigades developed into a highly structured organization. It had cells of regional leadership, with operations commanders and even financial officers. It also had intelligence-gathering operations and safe houses (hideouts). Possibly as many as four hundred full-time Red Brigades operatives worked underground with secret identities. More than one thousand supporters lived "above ground." Some supporters were the children of rich Italians seeking adventure. But some were former student revolutionaries who, by the mid-1970s, were themselves affluent industrialists, government workers, and politicians who secretly supported radical politics.

Red Brigades founder Renato Curcio is shown behind bars during his 1978 trial in Turin, Italy. Curcio was charged with forming an armed group for the purposes of subverting the Italian government.

SILENCING WITNESSES

The Red Brigades' favorite tactic of intimidating potential witnesses or informants was kneecapping. Red Brigades operatives would shoot a victim in the knee at close range, shattering the kneecap. Excruciatingly painful, the practice was also permanently crippling.

Along with intimidating witnesses, the Red Brigades also targeted police officers, politicians, judges, wardens, and correction officers with kidnappings, assassinations, and kneecappings. The group's objectives were simple: to frighten members of the legal system enough to prevent them from participating in court cases against Red Brigades leaders. ■

Most of the Red Brigades' attacks targeted symbols of Italy's establishment, such as union officials, politicians, businesspeople, and NATO commanders. The Red Brigades also voiced violent opposition to Italy's membership in NATO and to the presence of U.S. forces at military bases on Italian soil.

As part of their strategy, the Red Brigades wanted to commit acts of political violence that made all Italians feel threatened. The Italian authorities would be forced to respond by imposing strict security measures. One of the classic objectives of terrorism is to force a ruling government to take repressive counterterrorist measures. These measures include arrests without probable cause, widespread wiretapping and surveillance, and harsh interrogations of suspects and witnesses. When innocent citizens are caught up in these repressive security measures, a backlash against the government typically occurs. The backlash may even lead to the government's downfall.

Repression at the hands of security forces was a sensitive issue in Italy because of the country's Fascist history. Most Italians wanted to forget the years of Mussolini's rule and Italy's alliance with Nazi Germany. Sweeping police powers and arrests on political charges hinted at a return to those dark days.

ALLIANCES

The Red Brigades received secret support from the Soviet Union and from European groups that shared similar ideologies. Much of its funding also came from illegal businesses, bank robberies, and donations from sympathizers.

Like many of the era's European terrorist groups, the Red Brigades wanted a global revolution. They formed alliances with other terrorist organizations operating in the Mediterranean region, especially Palestinian groups. The Red Brigades-Palestinian alliance worked on a formula: the Palestinians provided the Italian terrorists with weapons, training, and shelter for Red Brigades operatives on the run. In exchange, the Red Brigades stored weapons in Italy for the Palestinians and participated in attacks against Israeli targets inside the country. But most of the actual cooperation between the Red Brigades and the Palestinian groups was gathering and sharing intelligence. ■

For this reason, the Italian authorities were in a difficult spot. They could not allow the Red Brigades to kill Italian officials in broad daylight. But they could not force witnesses, wary of the police and intimidated by the Red Brigades, to cooperate with authorities.

| ALDO MORO | The Red Brigades' most audacious—and subsequently infamous—attack was the kidnapping in Rome of former Italian premier Aldo Moro in March 1978. Moro was a leader of the Christian Democrats, a party long opposed to Communism. But Moro himself was known for working toward compromise and cooperation with the country's leftist parties.

■ ■

Moro's Kidnapping

Aldo Moro was on his way *to a special session of parliament, traveling with his usual detail of five bodyguards in two cars. Relaxing in the backseat with his newspaper, Moro looked up when his driver slammed on the brakes. Another car in front of them had stopped, and Moro's driver could not avoid hitting it. Moro might have thought it was nothing more than a fender bender, but his bodyguards could see that something much worse was happening. One guard lurched over the front seat and shoved Moro's head down just before gunfire engulfed the car. When the shooting stopped, all five bodyguards were dead. Moro was dragged from the backseat.*

Days later, a photograph of Moro looking battered and frightened was distributed to Italian news agencies. His Red Brigades kidnappers announced that Moro would be tried as a political prisoner and executed unless fifteen Red Brigades terrorists— including founder and military chieftain Renato Curcio, then on trial in Italy—were released.

For weeks Italian police conducted a haphazard search for Moro, while the government refused to negotiate with the Red Brigades or release any Red Brigades prisoners. The decision had tragic results. Aldo Moro's body was found stuffed in a car trunk on a Roman street near the Christian Democrats headquarters.

■ ■

Aldo Moro's kidnapping horrified and angered the Italian public. The Italian parliament empowered Giulio Andreotti as acting prime minister to respond to the Red Brigades. Andreotti pulled together a far-reaching parliamentary coalition that, for the first time in Italian history, included the Communist Party. The government enacted stern measures against political terrorism and formed the Nucleo Operativo Centrale di Sicurezza (Central Security Operation Unit or NOCS), a national counterterrorism commando unit. Parliament gave police new powers

Italians demonstrate against Red Brigades violence after the kidnapping and murder of former prime minister Aldo Moro. Moro was a popular political figure and expected by many to be the next president of Italy.

permitting large-scale arrests and even the right to shoot terrorist suspects who resisted arrest. The police rounded up thousands of suspects, many of whom were later convicted in special tribunals (courts).

The Italian judicial system also created a program called Repentance. Under this aggressive program, imprisoned Red Brigades operatives were able to trade lengthy sentences for complete confessions and information on their organization.

| THE END OF THE YEARS OF THE GUN | Pursued

and hunted, the Red Brigades moved even farther underground. But a new generation of leadership was gathering and soon managed to strike again. The kidnapping of NATO officer James Dozier, however, proved to be the Red Brigades' last major operation.

■ ■

Operation Winter Harvest

December 17, 1981. *When U.S. Army brigadier general James Dozier opened the door to his Verona, Italy, apartment, he thought he was letting in plumbers. It was late afternoon, and the men in the hallway claimed they needed to fix a bathroom leak that was seeping into the apartment below. Once inside, though, the men beat Dozier to the floor, stuffed him into a trunk, and took him away. His wife was left bound and gagged.*

Ten days later, a photo of the abducted general clutching a dated newspaper and a list of demands were broadcast around the world. Italian police officials, fearing that they had another Moro disaster on their hands, were determined to rescue Dozier. With U.S. support, Italian forces organized Operation Winter Harvest to locate Dozier.

Counterterrorist police regroup in front of a Padua, Italy, apartment building during Operation Winter Harvest in January 1982.

By late January 1982, Operation Winter Harvest had pinpointed an apartment in the Italian city of Padua.

Late in the morning on January 28, 1982, a moving van pulled up outside the Padua apartment building. The street was noisy with traffic and nearby construction. The kidnappers never heard the NOCS commandos jump down from the van and run up the stairs. The commandos had kicked in the apartment door before the kidnappers realized what was happening. Dozier was rescued just as he was about to be executed by one of his Red Brigades captors.

■ ■

By the early 1980s, police pressure and public disgust with the Red Brigades' violent tactics brought an end to the "Years of the Gun," as the group's reign of terror was known. Their international alliances faltered, and without a supply of money or safe havens abroad, the group was doomed. Internally, the Red Brigades had grown away from their working-class base and political purpose. By the early 1990s, the Red Brigades' message—and their violence—seemed outdated.

■ ■

Rising Again?

The train ride on the Intercity Express *from Rome to Florence usually takes just under two hours. Regular business travelers talk on their cell phones and type on their laptop computers. Some read the sports pages, hoping for encouraging news about Rome's chances in upcoming soccer games. As commuters read and work, the* carabinieri, *Italy's national police, move through the intercity train checking identity cards and passports.*

The carabinieri had begun routinely patrolling the trains after the September 11, 2001, al-Qaeda attacks in the United States and the arrest of several members of al-Qaeda terrorist cells in Italy. Security was even tighter in early 2003, with the onset of the U.S.-led war against Iraq. There was fear that Middle East terrorists were planning revenge attacks.

But as the carabinieri officers came to the second-class train cabin on March 2, 2003, they had no idea they were walking into a battle with two homegrown terrorists—Red Brigades operatives on assignment. At the sight of the police, Nadia Desdemona Lioce and Mario Galesi pulled out semiautomatic handguns and opened fire. One of the officers was killed by the fusillade. Galesi was killed when the officers returned fire. Lioce was apprehended.

Italian police escort Red Brigades member Paolo Persichetti from police headquarters in Turin, Italy, in August 2002. While hiding in France, Persichetti was convicted for the murders of two Italian government officials during the 1980s.

But offshoots of the group still trouble Italy's security and intelligence services. The police shootout on the train to Florence in 2003 was ominous. It followed some high-profile assassinations in recent years for which Red Brigades offshoots had claimed responsibility. It may be that Italy's homegrown terrorists are back in business.

Alexandros Giotopoulos: a Paris-born Greek intellectual considered the ideological leader of Revolutionary Movement 17 November

EAM-ELAS: two Greek resistance groups formed during World War II. EAM, the Greek acronym for the National Liberation Front, was a political organization. ELAS, the Greek acronym for National People's Liberation Army, was its military division.

European Union (EU): an organization of European countries formed to promote political and economic cooperation among members. The EU succeeded the European Economic Community or Common Market (1957–1967) and the European Community (1967–1991).

Georgios Papadopoulos: a colonel in the Greek army who led the military takeover of the country in 1967

November 17, 1973: the date of an antigovernment uprising of Greek students on an Athens university campus that was put down violently by the Greek army. Revolutionary Organization 17 November was named in remembrance of the day.

Pan-Hellenic Socialist Party: Greece's dominant political party

Revolutionary Organization 17 November: a Marxist-Leninist terrorist group founded in Greece in the early 1970s

GREECE:
REVOLUTIONARY ORGANIZATION 17 NOVEMBER

The seeds of communist revolution in Greece were sown during World War II, when the country was attacked by Italy, then occupied by the Nazis. Fierce resistance movements against the invaders soon sprang up, and the countryside became a guerrilla battlefield. Support for the resistance came mostly from Great Britain, where King George II of Greece had fled. King George hoped to reclaim his throne at the end of the war with the help of

A German military convoy rolls past a group of peasants in the Greek countryside in May 1941. The German occupation of Greece inspired a fierce resistance force of farmers, students, and working-class Greeks.

the Allies. But the Soviets were helping the resistance in their own way. Greece became a target of Soviet plans to establish a Communist government there. With the help of Soviet agents, Communist resistance groups fought German soldiers with effective hit-and-run attacks.

■ ■

The Greek Resistance

The best time to hit a German convoy in 1942 *was before dawn. The Germans expected the Greek resistance guerrillas to be back up in the hills by then, scattering to their hideouts before it got light. But the resistance knew the German sentries would be less alert in the early hours. If all went well, the guerrillas would get past the sentries and be close enough to the road to plant their British-supplied explosives.*

In a successful ambush, the explosions destroyed the first and last trucks in the convoy. The guerrillas machine-gunned everything

Greek resistance fighters, in military uniforms and traditional dress, pose after the liberation of Greece in 1944.

in between. After the smoke cleared, the guerrillas came out from their ambush positions to paint Communist symbols on the destroyed German vehicles, just to let the Nazi command know who was responsible for the attack. By the time word got out that the convoy had been hit, the resistance fighters would be back up in the hills.

Living in the mountains and hiding in caves wasn't easy. Food was scarce and the weapons the guerrillas carried were often pried from the hands of dead Germans. But the resistance was bound together by a cause. Free time was spent studying the works of Marx and Lenin, learning Communist ideology, and singing Communist folk songs. After the Nazi invaders were driven from the country, the guerrillas would be prepared to wage their own war of national liberation to establish a Communist utopia in Greece.

■ ■

By 1944 both Italy and Germany had withdrawn from Greece. The two most prominent guerrilla groups fought for control of the freed country. The Communist National Liberation Front-National People's Liberation Army (EAM-ELAS) set up a provisional (temporary) government in opposition to the Greek Democratic National Army (EDES).

| CIVIL WAR AND THE JUNTA | Although neither
EAM-ELAS nor EDES wanted King George II as their country's leader, they agreed in 1944 to allow the king to return. But the king's government immediately tried to break up the Communist EAM-ELAS. Fighting developed between EAM-ELAS and government troops backed by British forces. In 1945, after fierce fighting, EAM-ELAS agreed to disband ELAS, its military wing, if EAM were allowed to run candidates in elections. The government agreed, but government paramilitary forces still took action to destroy the Communist organization. When King George II died in 1946, a full-scale civil war erupted.

The United States, as part of its anti-Communist policy called the Truman Doctrine, came to the defense of the Greek government. U.S. military advisers and supplies were rushed into Greece. The battles between U.S.-backed government forces and the Communist guerrillas were fierce. Thousands were massacred on both sides, villages were burned, and entire families were torn apart.

The civil war ended in 1949 with the Communists' defeat. The Greek government set up reforms, and the economy recovered. But a bitter legacy lingered. A violent right wing emerged, especially inside the Greek military. They were angry about the bloodshed and misery the Communists had inflicted on the Greek people during the civil war. The Communists, for their part, could not forgive the United States and Great Britain for their support of the Greek government during the conflict.

Tensions between Greece's military right wing and the Communists came to a head in 1967. A group of military officers, fearful of gains the left wing had made in recent elections, seized control of the country. Colonel Georgios Papadopoulos led the junta, or military takeover. The junta was not popular and remained in power only through terror. Papadopoulos suspended the constitution, established a secret police force, and instituted the use of torture. Many European countries refused to deal with the junta because of its human rights abuses. The United States, however, viewed Greece as a crucial part of NATO's defense network and would not risk alienating the junta. The Communists and the political left wing never forgave the United States for that decision.

In the fall of 1973, large-scale student demonstrations openly challenged the junta's power. The Greek economy was in a shambles, and the country's mood supported radical political change. Students occupied the National Polytechnic University of Athens and called for citizens to rise up against the government. The army responded with brute force. On November 17, 1973, tanks assaulted the student-held campus. Hundreds were killed and wounded.

| 17 NOVEMBER IS BORN | Although the junta would fall the following year, the bloodletting of November 1973 was a call to arms for the country's radical Communist forces, from which came Revolutionary Organization 17 November. Many inside Greece's left-wing and Communist political parties believed that U.S. spies had worked with the Greek military to crush the November 1973 student uprising in Athens. This belief heightened 17 November's anti-imperialist, anti-Western, and vehemently anti-American ideology. The group announced that its goal was to establish a socialist state in Greece and to sever all ties to the United States, NATO, and the European Union (EU).

The Athens campus of the National Polytechnic University is littered with burned-out cars and debris on November 20, 1973, three days after the Greek military's violent put-down of a student demonstration.

17 November began its offensive by assassinating U.S. officials in Greece, such as embassy employees and military officers. In 1975 the group also began assassinating Greek officials. Seven of the victims were shot with the same .45-caliber handgun. With the use of a signature weapon, 17 November left its stamp on each assassination. The group began bombings in the 1980s, and a series of attacks was staged against American businesses in Greece. During the Persian Gulf War (1990–1991), 17 November's attacks against U.S. military targets increased.

To further the group's anti-EU mission, 17 November bombed Dutch, French, and German commercial and diplomatic targets and EU facilities. 17 November continued to direct violence at its own government, especially targeting economic offices and officials. In most of these attacks, civilian workers and passersby were killed or wounded.

British interests in Greece also came under attack. Many radical Greek leftists felt that Britain's support for George II at the end of the World War II had created many of Greece's postwar problems. 17 November strikes against the British include an unsuccessful mortar attack against the aircraft carrier *Ark Royal* in the Greek port of Piraeus in 1994.

Perhaps the most serious 17 November crime in recent years was the June 2000 assassination of Brigadier Stephen Saunders, the British military attaché shot dead as he sat in an Athens traffic jam.

The murder of Brigadier Saunders proved to be the beginning of the end for 17 November. Saunders was a British subject, and British police were allowed to take a leading role in investigating the crime. Investigators vowed not to leave Athens until Saunders's murderers were found. In 2002, while in police custody, 17 November operative Savvas Xiros admitted to the murder.

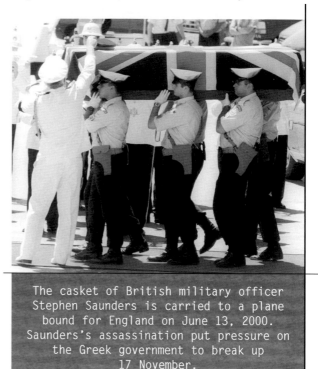

The casket of British military officer Stephen Saunders is carried to a plane bound for England on June 13, 2000. Saunders's assassination put pressure on the Greek government to break up 17 November.

| **FIGHTING 17 NOVEMBER** | For nearly thirty years, 17 November operated freely inside Greece. During that time, the group committed more than one hundred acts of terrorism—mostly murders and bombings. Yet Greek authorities never arrested a single 17 November operative. This lack of success raised the suspicion among U.S. and British officials that Greece's dominant political group, the Pan-Hellenic Socialist Party, sheltered 17 November. Under pressure from the United States and Britain, Greece intensified its efforts to curtail 17 November's violence.

■ ■

A Bombing Gone Wrong

Savvas Xiros *was one of the many 17 November operatives who managed to elude Greek authorities for decades. He would have never been caught had the bomb he was carrying not exploded prematurely on a Greek island in June 2002. The blast blew the lid off the secrecy and apathy that had kept 17 November one of the most covert terrorist organizations in the world.*

After the explosion, Greek police found Xiros's apartment keys. In searching his home, they found the signature .45-caliber gun used in 17 November attacks. From his hospital bed, a badly wounded Xiros confessed his membership in the organization and his part in the murder of British military officer Stephen Saunders. He also began naming names, and within weeks, much of 17 November's leadership was in custody, connected to a string of attacks and assassinations dating back to 1975.

■ ■

By July 2002, Greek police had arrested the group's ideological leader Alexandros Giotopoulos and its chief assassin Dimitris Koufodinas. This led to the apprehension of many more 17 November operatives.

Early in 2003, nineteen defendants went on trial in Athens, accused of having been active members of 17 November. As the organization's leader, Giotopoulos alone faces one thousand charges stemming from every

Greek counterterrorist police clear news photographers from an Athens street after discovering a 17 November hideout in July 2002. The 2002 police crackdown resulted in the arrests of many 17 November operatives and the discovery of a large stash of weapons.

attack attributed to 17 November. Some defendants have admitted participating in specific operations. Others admit membership in 17 November but will not take criminal responsibility for what they claim are political actions. Still others claim that the entire trial is a sham and that they are innocent victims of a political conspiracy. Greek prosecutors will use police findings (such as weapons stashes), DNA testing, and

TERRORISTS WITH DAY JOBS

17 November's leadership was largely homegrown and self-taught. There was little evidence of links to foreign terrorist groups, even those sharing similar ideologies. What actually made the leaders so difficult to crack were their links to each other. Many of those arrested in the July 2002 sweeps were related, by blood or marriage. The support and sympathy 17 November had from the Pan-Hellenic Socialist Party only strengthened these internal bonds.

But for all the group's Mafia-like blood ties and covert political support, perhaps what worked most in their favor was the fact that they were all so ordinary. They escaped police scrutiny by leading seemingly normal lives. Savvas Xiros was a religious-icon painter and the son of a Greek Orthodox priest. Dimitris Koufodinas was a beekeeper. Other operatives and assassins were, by day, schoolteachers, shopkeepers, civil servants, and real estate agents. Only Alexandros Giotopoulos, a French-born academic and son of a well-known Soviet-style Communist, fit the profile for the "usual suspects." ■

Brothers *(left to right)* Christodoulos, Savvas, and Vassilis Xiros are pictured in a 2000 Greek police handout. The close family relationships of 17 November operatives may be one reason counterterrorists had difficulty infiltrating the organization.

fingerprinting as evidence. About 450 witnesses are also expected to testify for both the prosecution and the defense. If convicted, most of the defendants face life in prison for multiple murders.

The Greek government considers 17 November to be defunct and its efforts to derail modern Greek democracy a failure. But some counterterrorists, members of the media, and victims' families have questioned why it took twenty-seven years for any 17 November operative to be brought to trial, suggesting that the group's terrorist war came close to success.

Fusako Shigenobu: the founder of the Japanese Red Army

imperialism: a practice in which powerful nations attempt to invade or take control of smaller, weaker countries to create an empire

Japanese Red Army (JRA): a Marxist-Leninist terrorist organization formed in Japan in the 1960s

nationalism: a political movement in which a nation claims the primary loyalty of a community of people

Popular Front for the Liberation of Palestine (PFLP): a terrorist group founded in the Middle East in 1967 to establish a socialist Palestinian state

Vietnam War: from 1959 to 1975, the military struggle for control of Vietnam, a Southeast Asian country

Zengakuren: the All-Japan Federation of Student Self-Governing Associations, a Communist student organization founded in Japan in 1948

JAPAN:
THE RED ARMY (JRA)

Japan has had a small but very organized Communist Party—the Japanese Communist Party (JCP)—since the 1920s. During the 1930s, however, a group of right-wing, ultranationalistic radicals, many from Japan's military, grew in influence. They used violent tactics, including assassinations, to pursue their political aims. They also expanded the territories belonging to the Japanese Empire by invading Manchuria, China, and other Pacific nations, actions that fueled the eruption of World War II. Many Japanese Communists who protested these imperialist invasions were arrested and executed by the right-wing radicals.

Japanese civilians line up for food at a distribution center in September 1945. For many, the country's defeat in World War II was humiliating, and life in the first few postwar years was difficult.

Japan surrendered in World War II after the Allies dropped two atomic bombs on Japan in August 1945. The bombings devastated the country psychologically. The Japanese people feared that the Allies might inflict more catastrophes if their government did not change. Democratic reforms and Communism both seemed to offer legitimate alternatives to imperialism and extreme nationalism. As a result, the JCP regained some political power, while U.S.-style democratic reforms reshaped the country. After the war, the United States had stepped in to help rebuild the country as a strong democratic nation and Western ally. Japan's economy began to flourish, and the country's government became a parliamentary system under the protection of the United States. The Japanese emperor, while more of a figurehead, was still nominally head of the nation.

REVERSE COURSE

After World War II, the U.S.-led occupation's plans for the recovery and reconstruction of Japan fit with most left-wing political thought. Japan's colonial empire was dissolved, and its military was disbanded. A new constitution reduced the emperor to a symbolic leader and extended the right to vote to all Japanese adults, including women. Land reforms and a labor union movement were encouraged to ensure that farmers and the working class shared in the economic recovery. Communists and leftists were welcomed in political debates.

But in the 1950s, as the Cold War heated up, U.S. policy changed to reflect its growing concern with the spread of Communism. This shift became known as reverse course. Under reverse course, the occupation encouraged the growth of capitalist corporations to quickly stabilize the Japanese economy. An economically successful society would be much less likely to turn to Communism. The occupation also tried to break up Communist groups and began promoting conservative organizations. The policies of reverse course brought the occupation and the United States in direct conflict with Japan's political left. ■

As the Cold War began in the 1950s, the United States wanted Japan's commitment in the global fight against Communism. A large part of the Japanese government favored an anti-Communist alliance with the United States. But many Japanese citizens wanted the country to simply remain neutral in the Cold War. They did not want Japan to sign treaties with either the United States or the USSR.

The JCP faced a simpler decision. As Communists, JCP members did not want to side with the United States and its capitalist allies. The JCP received moral and logistical guidance from the Soviet Union. But beyond the political conflict, the JCP felt that the U.S. presence in Japan was a continuation of the country's defeat in World War II. Honor is an important concept in Japanese society, and the JCP felt that the postwar U.S. occupation only further humiliated the Japanese people.

| **STUDENT REVOLTS** | By the 1960s, Japan's economy was booming, and the living standard for most Japanese was far better than ever before. Communists had difficulty arguing for radical social change. Japanese society was also very rigid and the work ethic very strong. Duty to one's family and allegiance to one's company far outweighed Marxist ideology.

This 1964 photo of Tokyo teenagers in Western clothes reflects the influence of Western popular culture. Some Japanese felt this influence came at the expense of their own culture.

The one place where Communism found a foothold was on Japan's college campuses. The Communists were very strong inside the Zengakuren, or the All-Japan Federation of Student Self-Governing Associations, one of the largest organizations in Japan. At one time, nearly 60 percent of all the country's students belonged to the Zengakuren. The pro-Communist ideologies held by many students had begun as a protest against their educational system's close links with corporate success. The middle-class "company man" had become the ideal in Japanese society, and a college degree was increasingly treated as a career move. Communist students objected to using education only as a moneymaking strategy.

In the 1960s, Tokyo was the site of serious student uprisings, many of them extremely violent. Zengakuren's protests had moved beyond educational reform to issues that troubled students in the United States and Europe. The Zengakuren voiced opposition to the Vietnam War and to Japan's close ties with the United States. Students also opposed the emperor, still a revered figure in traditional Japanese life. These radical protests appealed to many left-wing students. The protests

Tokyo police battle rioting members of the Zengakuren in April 1960. The students were protesting Japan's ratification of its anti-Communist security treaty with the United States.

not only supported the students' politics, but they provided a group to belong to, in a culture where individualism was not the norm.

Soviet intelligence services supported the Japanese left-wing radicals. At the same time, North Korea, a communist country with an authoritarian leader, was eager to destabilize Japan, one of the most important U.S. allies in the Pacific. Japanese radicals became North Korea's tools for sabotage.

Among the students who became attracted to left-wing politics and terrorist violence was Fusako Shigenobu. She founded the Japanese Red Army (JRA) in the late 1960s and envisioned the overthrow of the government and monarchy to establish a Marxist Socialist People's Republic of Japan.

In the male-dominated world of terrorism, Fusako Shigenobu was unique. Nicknamed the "Red Queen," she grew up in poverty and nursed a resentment over Japan's humiliation in World War II. Shigenobu put much of the blame for her country's shame on the presence of the United States in Japan.

Young, beautiful, and elegant, Shigenobu was able to recruit male operatives and to enlist international support for the JRA. And she was ruthless. Under Shigenobu's leadership, the JRA was one of the first terrorist groups—secular or religious—to practice suicide attacks.

Global ambitions brought Shigenobu to the Middle East, where she could evade the Japanese intelligence service and get her recruits military and terrorist training. With the help of the North Koreans, Soviets, and Syrians, Shigenobu established an international alliance with the Popular Front for the Liberation of Palestine (PFLP). The PFLP was headquartered in Lebanon, and the JRA sent its most capable operatives there for training. They learned how to build bombs, stage aircraft hijackings, and carry out assassinations.

■ ■

Inside a Terrorist Training Camp

The groups could not express *their pleasure at working together. The Palestinian instructors did not speak Japanese, and the Japanese pupils knew no Arabic. But the four men and four women undergoing advanced demolitions training had not come this far for compliments and slaps on the back. Wearing tan fatigues with AK-47 rifles slung over their shoulders, the eight JRA operatives were learning to improvise explosive booby traps. Wiring the inside of a 747 passenger jet or an embassy with dynamite and plastic explosives required skill and speed—both could be learned at this Palestinian terrorist camp in Lebanon.*

The camp, near Sidon in southern Lebanon, was run by the PFLP and open to "exchange students" from all over the world. Germans, Irish, South Africans, and Kurds all crowded into the camp's dormitories. Instruction began at daybreak and ended in the early evening. Physical training began before the Mediterranean sun scorched the camp. Then students would be driven to a remote section of the camp to take target practice and learn to detonate explosives.

When the sun was at its hottest, training moved indoors. Classroom instruction included the secrets of the airline industry and international travel, document forgery, intelligence and counterintelligence, and advanced explosives. Field training in martial arts, executions, and sabotage techniques was reserved for the late afternoon, when the sun began its descent.

The different groups of foreign students in the camp interacted

*very little. The Japanese in particular kept to themselves. They never
ventured into Sidon to enjoy the local entertainments. Their
entertainment was planning the revolution.*

■ ■

The JRA operatives proved useful to their Middle Eastern
comrades. Unlike Palestinians, the Japanese were not regarded with
suspicion at airports and border crossings. Free to travel internationally, they
were ideally suited for attacking Israeli targets. On May 30, 1972, three
JRA terrorists landed at Lod Airport in Israel on a flight from Rome. At the
baggage claim area, they removed automatic weapons and hand grenades
from their suitcases and began firing. They killed twenty-six people, most of
them Puerto Ricans on a Christian pilgrimage. Another fifty travelers were
seriously wounded. Two of the terrorists were killed by Israeli police.
Shigenobu is believed to have planned the attack.

The Lod Massacre, however, was not the JRA's largest operation. In
July 1973, JRA and Lebanese guerrillas hijacked a Japan Airlines plane
over the Netherlands and diverted it to Libya. After releasing the
passengers and crew, the hijackers blew up the plane in a show of strength.

Bloodied luggage lies scattered in the Lod Airport in Tel Aviv, Israel,
after the JRA terrorist attack in May 1972. Most of those killed in the
attack were tourists from Puerto Rico visiting religious sites.

In September 1974, JRA operatives seized the French embassy in the Hague, the Netherlands' seat of government. The French ambassador was eventually freed in exchange for the release of jailed JRA members. The JRA also attempted to take over the U.S. embassy in Kuala Lumpur, Malaysia, in 1975. In September 1977, the JRA received a $6 million ransom after hijacking a Japan Airlines jet over India. In April 1988, Junzo Okudaira, a JRA operative, bombed a social club in Naples, Italy, killing five people, including a U.S. soldier. At the same time Okudaira was arrested in Italy, JRA operative Yu Kikumura was arrested in the United States. Stopped by police on the New Jersey Turnpike, Kikumura was found with explosives in his car, apparently planning an attack to coincide with the bombing of the Naples social club.

Japanese Red Army leader Fusako Shigenobu is shown after her November 2000 arrest in Osaka, Japan. Shigenobu was a fugitive from Japanese police for almost thirty years.

In the 1990s, the JRA's membership and support declined. Several JRA operatives were arrested in Japan and the United States, while Shigenobu and others remained in Lebanon. There is evidence that the remaining JRA was planning to set up bases in North Korea, the Philippines, and Singapore, but they did not claim responsibility for any terrorist attacks after the Naples bombing.

The JRA was dealt its final blows as the new century began. In March 2000, Lebanon deported four JRA members after coming to agreement with the Japanese government. In November 2000, Special Weapons and Tactics (SWAT) teams from the Japanese police raided a hotel in Osaka, arresting Fusako Shigenobu on charges of terrorism and passport fraud. It is unknown how many JRA members remain at large, but in 2002, the U.S. State Department removed the group from its list of active terrorist organizations.

cocaine: an addictive drug made from the South American coca shrub. According to the U.S. Drug Enforcement Administration, organized crime groups in Colombia control the world's supply of cocaine.

Fidel Castro: Communist leader of Cuba, an island nation in the Caribbean Sea, since 1959

Latin America: the countries of the Western Hemisphere south of the United States, from Mexico to South America. The region is called Latin America because it refers to nations that developed from the colonies of France, Spain, and Portugal, all countries with Latin-based languages.

La Violencia: the Colombian civil war that raged from 1948 to 1958

Manuel Marulanda: founder of the Revolutionary Armed Forces of Colombia (FARC)

Revolutionary Armed Forces of Colombia (FARC): a left-wing organization formed in 1966 as the armed militia of the Colombian Communist Party

COLOMBIA:
REVOLUTIONARY ARMED FORCES OF COLOMBIA
(FARC)

Communism, with its promise of equal distribution of wealth and power, has long had strong appeal in Latin America. Many of the region's nations are rich in natural resources such as oil, minerals, and forests. Only a small portion of society gets the benefits, however, and the gap between the rich and the poor is enormous. In some countries, as much as 95 percent of a nation's wealth belongs to less than 1 percent of the population. And at the bottom of the economic heap are rural peasants, whom the Communists see as a symbol of the brutality and inequality of capitalism and colonialism.

Political power in Latin America also has been unequally distributed and usually lays in the hands of rich landowners, industrialists, and military officers. As a result, the ideas and institutions of democracy—freedom of the press, protection of voters' rights, and elected officials and lawmakers—have often been corrupted or weak. In this climate, Communist ideology and violent struggle have found fertile ground.

Three additional factors also explain the rise of Communist rebels in the region. First, the United States has always played an aggressive role in Latin American politics, government, and economics. For example, the United States controlled the Panama Canal, and American corporations bought up much of the profitable land. The poor and politically oppressed in these countries have thus often linked their downtrodden economic and human rights situations to the United States, the world's most powerful capitalist democracy.

Second, the Roman Catholic Church, an important social institution in Latin America, has often criticized the repressive measures taken by landowners and military police against native peoples. This outspoken criticism has often linked the political purposes of the Communists and the church, even though their ideologies are far apart on most issues.

The third important factor in the development of Latin American Communist terrorist groups was the rise to power of Fidel Castro in Cuba. When Castro took power in Cuba in 1959, he established a Marxist government and embraced the Soviet Union as an ally. This brought the Cold War to the Western Hemisphere. The USSR began making plans to spread Communism throughout Central and South America. One of the early objects of Soviet interest was Colombia.

Fidel Castro *(standing center)* and members of his top command are pictured in the Cuban jungle in June 1967. Castro's success in seizing power in Cuba in 1959 inspired many Latin American Communist rebels.

Colombia is the fourth largest country in South America, occupying the continent's northwestern corner. The country contains grasslands, tropical rain forests, and the Amazon River basin. In the west, the Andes Mountains dominate the terrain. Most of Colombia's cities and towns, including the capital Bogotá, lie in Andean plateaus and valleys. The mountainous regions are the traditional home of Colombia's peasants, who work the land.

By 1959 Colombia had just survived a ten-year civil war known as

La Violencia (the Violence), in which the country's two main political parties, the Liberals and the Conservatives, had competed for control of the government. Some 200,000 Colombians had been killed, and raiding and looting had been widespread.

Eventually, Liberal and Conservative leaders came up with a plan to share power. But the seeds of political revolt had been planted. By the 1960s, many of the Liberals who had radically opposed the government during La Violencia had turned to Communism.

| FARC's Beginnings |

In the 1960s, university students, Catholic radicals, and left-wing intellectuals in Colombia hoped to copy the success of Fidel Castro's revolution in Cuba. They founded several Communist organizations, the most fanatical of which was the Fuerzas Armadas Revolucionarios de Colombia (Revolutionary Armed Forces of Colombia, or FARC). FARC dedicated itself to overthrowing the Colombian government and to installing a left-wing Marxist-Leninist politburo (government body).

Manuel "Sureshot" Marulanda formed FARC in 1966 as the armed militia of the Colombian Communist Party. Early FARC activities included raiding military posts, from which the group obtained weapons,

Women make up about 30 percent of FARC's guerrilla force. They carry the same weapons as and fight alongside their male counterparts.

ammunition, and uniforms. FARC enjoyed tremendous logistical support from the Soviet Union and continues to be backed by Cuba.

FARC has recruited peasants and farmers in rural areas, where sympathy for Communist rebellion is strong. Many recruits are indigenous Indians from regional tribes. As a result, much of FARC's terrorist activity has taken place in the Colombian countryside.

■ ■

FARC Warriors

Unlike some South American guerrilla outfits, *FARC is a highly disciplined military organization spread over the Colombian countryside. The FARC army is divided into sixty combat battalions, which are subdivided into companies, platoons, and squads. A junior officer responsible to the field commanders heads each of those subdivisions.*

FARC guerrillas patrol a rural road. The sign in the background protests U.S. intervention in Latin America.

Life inside a FARC outpost resembles life at a smoothly run military base. Guards with orders to shoot to kill patrol the edges of the camp. Inside the garrison, the cabins, tents, and weapons collections are neat and orderly. Off duty, the guerrilla warriors play soccer, watch TV, and undergo political dedication classes where Marxist beliefs are hammered home.

Outside the camp, guerrillas on duty can be out in the field battling the Colombian military or bringing a rural village under their control. Guerrillas will often safeguard fields of coca and the transport areas where the crops are taken to be processed into cocaine.

■ ■

| FARC Activities |
Until the late 1980s, FARC's growth was slow. It was active mostly in the depths of the countryside, even into the jungle, where peasants eked out a living, largely ignored by the government. But in the 1980s, Colombia became a major supplier of cocaine to the United States and other wealthy countries. When FARC discovered the drug trade, it found an endless supply of cash. FARC muscled in on cocaine trafficking to finance its war against the government in Bogotá.

According to the U.S. Drug Enforcement Administration, FARC is involved in every aspect of the drug business. From processing cocaine and heroin to charging drug runners a hefty fee for using airstrips, FARC controls the industry. The group's yearly profits from the cocaine trade are estimated to be hundreds of millions of dollars.

FARC discovered another profitable criminal activity in the 1980s—ransom kidnapping. The group targets wealthy landowners, foreign tourists, and prominent international and domestic officials. Often, though, the targets of the violence are unfortunate businesspeople

ANTI-AMERICANISM

One of the tenets of FARC's war in Colombia has been its anti-American doctrine. Because of its Communist ideology, FARC has always viewed the United States as its enemy. The Colombian military—supported by massive U.S. aid and ground support, including the assistance of U.S. Special Forces—has been battling FARC for more than thirty years. Efforts to disrupt FARC activities have centered on the cocaine trade, the lifeblood of FARC's control. U.S. law enforcement and military personnel actively assist Colombian government forces fighting against drug operations. Confrontations between the rebel army and the U.S. antidrug forces have become regular and violent. ■

cornered on isolated rural highways or caught inside backwater hotels.

Once boasting more than fifteen thousand soldiers, FARC controlled over one-third of the nation and had a presence virtually everywhere. In the 1990s, it defeated the Colombian army on a regular basis, capturing several hundred security force officers. In 1998, hoping to gain some control over the situation, the Colombian government gave FARC control of four counties in south central Colombia. These rural areas were meant as safe havens for FARC, where they would not be pursued by government soldiers, but critics argued that FARC only used the land to ex-pand its drug-trafficking industry.

FARC also has favored assassinations and hijackings to promote its goals and political aspirations. In February 2002, for example, FARC

A FARC guerrilla sets fire to ballots in a mountain village during the 2002 presidential elections. Disrupting voting is one FARC strategy for discouraging opposition to the group's control in rural regions.

terrorists hijacked a domestic commercial flight and kidnapped a Colombian senator who was a passenger. FARC has also frequently attacked oil pipelines and other business targets, crippling the country's economic infrastructure.

THE END OF A PEACE PROCESS? | Over the years,
FARC and the Colombian government have attempted truces to end the violence. Both sides have claimed that peace accords have been broken or ignored by the other.

In 2002 the Colombian government called off peace negotiations after three years of unproductive talks. Then-president Andres Pastrana sent in army troops to take back FARC-controlled safe havens. Battles between the guerrillas and regular army increased. More political kidnappings and assassinations took place, as well as more bombings and hijackings.

The Colombian government claims that FARC has become nothing more than a drug-trafficking and terrorist organization, no longer standing for social justice for Colombian peasants. Polls have shown that general support for FARC in rural areas has dropped to a small percentage. FARC's credibility with the peasant population was further damaged in May 2002, when the group purposely bombed a church in western Colombia in which 119 villagers were hiding from a gun battle.

Colombian citizens demonstrate in favor of continued negotiations between the government and FARC in January 2002. The sign carried by the man at the right reads, "Peace" in Spanish.

In August 2002—as new president, Alvaro Uribe, was being inaugurated—a FARC mortar attack in a poor Bogotá neighborhood killed twenty-one people. FARC executed ten hostages in May 2003, after the government attempted to rescue some of the dozens of Colombian officials, police officers, and soldiers FARC holds hostage.

In retaliation for the government reclaiming the safe havens, the group has indicated that it will move its terrorist attacks from the countryside to Colombian cities, causing more civilian causalities. FARC leadership continues to claim its commitment to Marxist socialist reform. But if support for the guerrilla force sinks farther, FARC's rebels may find themselves with no one to fight for.

Abimael Guzmán: the founder of the Shining Path. Guzmán was captured by government forces and imprisoned in 1992

collective: a group that controls production and distribution of economic goods (such as food or factory products) for all the people

Maoism: a form of Communism named for Mao Zedong, China's head of state from 1949 to 1976. Chairman Mao combined Marxist-Leninist theory with Chinese political experience. In particular, Maoism advises beginning Communist revolutions in rural areas, a theory that has worked well for South American guerrilla groups.

Shining Path: a violent Peruvian terrorist group founded in the 1960s by Abimael Guzmán. The Shining Path is dedicated to Maoist Communism and to undermining the country's elected government.

Túpac Amaru II: a Peruvian Indian leader executed in the 1780s for rebelling against Spanish rule

Túpac Amaru Revolutionary Movement: a violent Peruvian terrorist group founded in 1983. Túpac Amaru is dedicated to Marxist-Leninist Communism and to undermining the country's elected government.

PERU:
THE SHINING PATH
AND TÚPAC AMARU
REVOLUTIONARY
MOVEMENT

Located along the Pacific Ocean in central western South America, Peru is the continent's third largest country. It lies just south of Colombia, and its landscape is also dominated by the Andes Mountains.

Peru was once the center of an empire ruled by a native people called the Incas. After European explorers brought back news of the Incas' enormous gold and silver mines, the empire became the target of Spanish greed. In the early sixteenth century, while the Inca Empire was weakened by civil conflicts, soldiers sent by the Spanish king took over the realm.

The king gave Spanish aristocrats large portions of land that held all the country's farming and mining wealth. The aristocrats forced Peruvian natives to work for little pay on the farms, in the mines, and as servants on their large estates, called haciendas. If the workers rebelled, they were jailed or beaten. Peru thus became a divided society, with an enormous gap between the Spanish-descended rich people and the poor native people. This pattern endured for centuries, even after Peru won its independence from Spain in the early nineteenth century.

After independence, power remained in the hands of people of Spanish heritage. A central government was established, but military takeovers were common. Economic problems such as serious inflation, national debt, and unemployment caused strikes and riots that further undermined the country's stability. By the 1900s, Peru's natural resources—including petroleum, copper, gold, silver, and iron—had attracted European and U.S. companies, but such trade only benefited Peru's rich and influential. The poor in Peru remained alienated.

In the mid-twentieth century, land reforms were passed that intended to return much of the farmland to native Peruvian peasants. The actual carrying out of these reforms, however, was bogged down in bureaucracy, and political power in rural areas remained in the hands of a few. Peasants invaded and seized many wealthy estates. To calm the situation, the government promised better reforms, but no actual improvements happened. The peasant class was again left angry and frustrated. The situation was ripe for exploitation by Communist groups that sought class warfare and rights for the rural poor.

Street vendors near a tourist site sell blankets, clothes, and food. Peru's economy has a large "informal sector" in which people grow or make items for local markets. Successful local businesspeople sometimes find themselves the target of Shining Path guerrillas seeking to control rural areas.

THE SHINING PATH

In the late 1960s, Abimael Guzmán founded the Shining Path (or Sendero Luminoso in Spanish) whose philosophy incorporates a brand of Communism called Maoism, after the Chinese Communist leader Mao Zedong. Maoism urges using a peasant population to begin a political revolution. This theory struck a chord with Guzmán, who knew Peru's peasants had already staged uprisings against the wealthy and powerful. Guzmán's eventual goal was to establish a rigid regime similar to China's, in which the state controls every aspect of day-to-day life. The individual is nothing; the state and the Communist collective is everything.

■ ■

Abimael Guzmán

Like other groups driven by Communist ideology, the Shining Path got its start on a college campus. Professor Abimael Guzmán founded the group at the University of San Cristobal del Huamanga in Ayacucho in the central highlands of Peru. Ayacucho is an isolated *area with many poor people. University students and teachers could see the oppression and poverty that surrounded them. Guzmán's own brand of fiery Communist ideology found a ready audience.*

Guzmán was a mysterious figure. His charisma was based more on his fanatic revolutionary zeal than on any personal appeal or actual accomplishments. Guzmán's version of Communism always included violence. It fed on the resentment of the rural poor and on the bitterness of local conflicts. And it allowed no dissent. When joining up, Shining Path members were required to sign a letter of loyalty not to the organization but to Guzmán.

■ ■

| SHINING PATH STRATEGIES | In 1980 the Shining

Path began its war against government forces by attacking a polling place (an official election voting site) in the Andean city of Ayacucho. By preventing citizens from exercising their right to vote, the Shining Path struck at order, communication, and national security. They also attacked small-time market traders, businesspeople, and local officials. By causing disorder, chaos, and fear, the group hoped to force the government's

Andean women, relatives of terrorism victims, demonstrate in Ayacucho, where Abimael Guzmán founded the Shining Path. Andean natives are the most frequent victims of guerrilla and counterinsurgency battles.

collapse. Into the resulting power vacuum would step the Shining Path.

As the group stepped up activities, ruthlessness became the Shining Path's calling card. Village chiefs and town council leaders who refused to support the revolution were often hacked to death with machetes. Anyone else resisting the Shining Path risked being tried at the group's own mock courts in the jungle. Guzmán's operatives forced villagers to witness the executions of those found guilty. Rural peasants began to realize that the Shining Path's violence only added to their troubles.

Involvement in the drug trade increased the Shining Path's ruthlessness. Peru is the second largest producer of cocaine in the world after Colombia. To support its antigovernment campaign, the Shining Path collected "taxes" from drug traffickers. These taxes became the group's main source of income.

The Shining Path also resorted to murders, kidnappings, political extortions, and bombings to advance their cause. The worst single incident happened in July 1992, when two car bombs went off in a middle-class neighborhood in Lima, the Peruvian capital. Twenty people were killed, and more than 250 were injured.

Government forces pursuing Shining Path terrorists were often ambushed in the impassable jungles of the country. At one time, about five thousand Shining Path terrorists hid in the mountains and jungles of Peru.

Abimael Guzmán, founder of the Shining Path, is shown behind bars in a September 1992 photo.

COUNTERATTACK | In

September 1992, Peruvian authorities moved in on a Shining Path hideout in Lima. Abimael Guzmán and six other leaders were captured. Guzmán was tried by a military court and sentenced to life in prison, where he remains. From prison, Guzmán called on the group to agree to a cease-fire with the Peruvian government. But the cease-fire only caused a split in the Shining Path.

For its part, the government of Peru has often employed a brutal counterterrorism policy. Human rights activists accuse the Peruvian military of widespread human rights abuses in cracking down on terrorists. Peru's then president Alberto Fujimori's determination to crush the Shining Path even led to his suspending the Peruvian constitution. Fujimori claimed that the Shining Path was ruining Peru and that he could not fight the group through conventional means. But activists and governments throughout the world condemned Fujimori's use of wiretapping, secret trials, and the arrest of thousands of Peruvian citizens. The military's abuses can be added to the estimated thirty thousand deaths attributed to the Shining Path's war with the government.

After Guzmán's arrest, the number of active Shining Path members dropped to fewer than one thousand. The rebels have moved away from Lima and other Peruvian cities into unpopulated areas of the jungle. In 1999 police landed another serious blow to the terrorist group. They arrested Ramirez Durand (known as Feliciano), the man who had taken over the Shining Path leadership from Guzmán.

But the Shining Path has seemingly survived these setbacks. The group is suspected in a March 2002 car bombing near the U.S. embassy in Lima, two days before U.S. president George Bush's state visit. Following that attack, Peruvian president Alejandro Toledo announced plans to reconstruct the country's intelligence agencies and to double the budget for counterterrorism units. The strong response suggests that the Shining Path remains a threat.

| Túpac Amaru Revolutionary Movement |

Peru's other main Communist terrorist group is a sworn enemy of the Shining Path. Túpac Amaru Revolutionary Movement (Movimiento Revolucionario Túpac Amaru, or MRTA) is a Marxist-Leninist group inspired by Fidel Castro. Like the Shining Path, Túpac Amaru wants to replace Peru's capitalist government with a Communist regime. But to the Shining Path, the group has always been unfaithful to true Marxist ideology. So while the Shining Path and Túpac Amaru both fought to overthrow the government, the argument over the purity of each group's ideology prevented them from working together.

Much smaller than the Shining Path, Túpac Amaru was organized in 1983 by members of previous left-wing revolutionary groups.

Counterterrorist experts believe that Túpac Amaru never had more than two thousand members. One of the group's primary goals is to remove all foreign influence from the country. U.S. and other foreign embassies have been frequently targeted, especially in Lima. In 1991, during the Persian Gulf War, Túpac Amaru terrorists bombed the U.S. ambassador's Lima residence, killing two policemen. The group also took credit for bombing several government buildings and for many bank robberies, ambushes, kidnappings, and assassinations.

A Peruvian man holds a portrait of Túpac Amaru II, a Peruvian Indian executed in 1781 for rebelling against Spanish rule. Túpac Amaru Revolutionary Movement takes its named from the rebel hero.

In 1992 Túpac Amaru's top commander, Victor Polay, was arrested and sentenced to life in prison. Many other Túpac Amaru leaders surrendered their weapons to the Peruvian government. The group's membership dropped to just a few hundred, most of whom were believed to be hiding in the jungle.

Túpac Amaru's remaining leadership carried out the group's most infamous attack on December 17, 1996. Fourteen terrorists seized the Japanese ambassador's residence in Lima. The ambassador was hosting a reception, and Túpac Amaru took hundreds of guests hostage, including government ministers and members of the Peruvian legislature. Attacking the Japanese ambassador was significant because Peru's then president Alberto Fujimori was of Japanese descent. This was an attack not only against Fujimori's antiterrorism but also against Japanese influence in the country.

The terrorists demanded that the government release their imprisoned Túpac Amaru comrades. Peruvian officials began negotiations, and the terrorists released all but seventy-two of the hostages. But after four months of negotiations, no resolution had been reached. On April 22, 1997, President Fujimori ordered a raid on the ambassador's home. One hundred forty Peruvian commandos launched a well-planned and well-executed assault on the compound. To achieve the element of surprise, the commandos had dug tunnels underneath the compound and then breached walls and floors with powerful explosive charges. The commandos killed all the rebels. One hostage and two soldiers also died in the rescue raid.

Túpac Amaru guerrillas pose in the Peruvian jungle. Their banner carries a picture of the group's namesake, Túpac Amaru II, and the group's initials in Spanish.

Boredom Can Be Lethal

For the Túpac Amaru terrorists *and their hostages holed up together for four months inside the Japanese ambassador's residence, life became oddly mundane. For the hostages, the ordeal turned from fear, to anxiety, to boredom, to the resigned feeling of incarceration. Conditions inside the ambassador's luxurious home were not easy. The opulent mansion could have provided enormous comfort for the hostages. But they were forced to huddle together, always under the vigilant watch of the terrorists. Meals, trips to the bathroom, and bathing became laborious rites of permission and observation.*

For the terrorists, too, the takeover turned from excitement at their success to fear of an immediate counterattack. When nothing

Peruvian counterterrorist forces gather outside the Lima residence of the Japanese ambassador to Peru on April 22, 1997.

happened, the fear turned to resignation. Over the weeks, the guards became less vigilant. They were less likely to notice small noises or to keep their weapons ready.

On the afternoon of April 22, 1997, most of the terrorists were absorbed in their daily ritual—a post-lunch soccer game. With their weapons on a nearby couch, the terrorists were playing four-on-four, displaying their skill and passion for the national sport. But midgame, the walls and floors erupted in orange fireballs. Blinding black smoke and gunfire followed the explosions. The terrorists had allowed routine to dull their thinking. The Peruvian counterterrorist commandos used that to their advantage.

Most of Túpac Amaru's remaining leadership was killed in the embassy raid. Membership dropped to fewer than one hundred. While some terrorism experts worry that the Shining Path is regrouping, many have said they do not believe Túpac Amaru continues to be a threat to Peru.

EPILOGUE*

Some of the Communist terror groups profiled have ceased operations, lost their leaders to arrest, or no longer win local support. There are exceptions, however.

RED BRIGADES

The original organization is disbanded. But the assassinations of Italian government advisers in 1999 and 2002 and the 2003 shootout with police on an intercity train were all attributed to offshoots of the Red Brigades.

17 NOVEMBER

Some counterterrorists worry that one arm of 17 November sacrificed itself to mislead police into thinking they had caught the whole group in the 2002 sweep. Some top 17 November operatives remain at large, and police documents leaked to the media after the 2002 arrests suggest that 17 November had been planning a major operation. The 2004 Summer Olympic Games to be held in Athens remain a concern.

FARC

The Colombian terrorist group is still clearly in operation. The 2003 escalation of violence over the canceled peace talks suggests that FARC has no intention of giving up. After the May 2003 execution of nine FARC hostages, some Colombians urged President Alvaro Uribe to release jailed guerrillas in exchange for FARC's remaining hostages. But Uribe has said he will not consider such an exchange unless it is brokered by the United Nations. In June 2003, police captured thirty-four FARC rebels, including leaders of the group's urban militia. Uribe also deployed a newly trained force of 10,000 peasant soldiers to guard rural areas against leftist guerrillas and right-wing paramilitary groups.

SHINING PATH

Despite the group's loss of leadership and members, a resurgence of the Shining Path remains a threat. In June 2003, Peruvian soldiers rescued seventy-one construction workers who had been kidnapped while working on an oil pipeline in the Andes. President Alejandro Toledo blamed the Shining Path for the kidnappings, while insisting that terrorism is not on the rise again in Peru. ■

*Please note that the information contained in this book was current at the time of publication. To find sources for late-breaking news, please consult the websites listed on pages 68-69.

TIMELINE

Red Army Faction
Red Brigades
17 November
Japanese Red Army
FARC
Shining Path
Túpac Amaru

1922　The Union of Soviet Socialist Republics (USSR) is created.

1939-1945　World War II is fought.

1940　Benito Mussolini orders his troops into Greece.

1941　Adolf Hitler's German army invades Greece. The Greek Communist Party forms.

1944　Germany withdraws from Greece.

1946-1949　The Greek civil war is fought.

1948-1958　La Violencia, Colombia's civil war, is fought.

1949　The Greek civil war ends.

1959　Fidel Castro takes power in Cuba.

1966　The Revolutionary Armed Forces of Colombia (FARC) is formed.

1968　Students riot against the Vietnam War in Paris. In Germany, the Red Army Faction (RAF) sets fire to a department store.

1969　The Red Brigades is formed at an Italian university.

1972　The RAF launches a two-week terror campaign in Germany. Many RAF members are captured. Three Japanese Red Army (JRA) terrorists attack travelers at Israel's Lod Airport.

1973　The Greek military violently quells a student demonstration in Athens. JRA and Lebanese guerrillas hijack a Japan Airlines flight.

1975 17 November assassinates U.S. embassy employee Richard Welch and several Greek officials. The JRA attempts to take over the U.S. embassy in Kuala Lumpur, Malaysia.

1977 The RAF kidnaps West German businessman Hanns-Martin Schleyer. Several RAF leaders commit suicide in prison. The JRA hijacks a Japan Airlines flight.

1978 The Red Brigades kidnap and murder Italian politician Aldo Moro in Rome.

1980 The Shining Path destroys a polling place in Peru.

1981 The Red Brigades kidnap U.S. Army officer James Dozier in Verona.

1983 Túpac Amaru Revolutionary Movement forms in Peru. 17 November assassinates U.S. Navy captain George Tsantes.

1988 JRA operative Junzo Okudaira bombs a club for U.S. soldiers in Naples, Italy. 17 November assassinates U.S. military attaché William Nordeen.

1990 East and West Germany are reunified. 17 November attacks the Athens office of the European Community.

1991 The RAF attacks the U.S. embassy in Bonn, Germany. Túpac Amaru terrorists bomb the U.S. ambassador's residence in Lima, Peru.

1992 The Shining Path plants a car comb in a Lima neighborhood killing twenty people. Abimael Guzmán and other Shining Path leaders are captured.

1993 The Shining Path plants a car bomb outside the U.S. embassy in Lima.

1994 German counterterrorist police kill RAF commander Wolfgang Grams. 17 November claims responsibility for the unsuccessful bombing of the British aircraft carrier *Ark Royal*.

1996   Túpac Amaru rebels overtake the Lima residence of the Japanese ambassador to Peru.

1997   Peruvian counterterrorist commandos invade the Japanese ambassador's house in Lima, rescuing the hostages held by Túpac Amaru.

1998   The news agency Reuters receives a fax from RAF leaders announcing that the group is disbanding. Police in Lima arrest four Shining Path leaders.

1999   Italian government adviser Massimo D'Antona is murdered by a Red Brigades offshoot. Shining Path leader Ramirez Durand is captured in Peru.

2000   17 November operatives kill British military officer Stephen Saunders in Athens, Greece. In Colombia, FARC rebels repeatedly bomb sections of a major oil pipeline. JRA leader Fusako Shigenobu is arrested in Osaka, Japan.

2002   Italian official Marco Biagi is murdered by a Red Brigades offshoot. Greek police arrest 17 November suspects after a failed bombing. FARC operatives kidnap thirteen government officials. Colombian president Andres Pastrana calls off peace negotiations with FARC leadership.

2003   Nineteen 17 November defendants go on trial in Greece. Two Red Brigades terrorists are captured after a shootout with Italian police on a train. FARC executes ten hostages after a government attempt to rescue them.

SELECTED BIBLIOGRAPHY

Alexander, Yonah, and Dennis A. Pluchinsky. *European Terrorism Today and Tomorrow*. McLean, VA: Brassey's US, 1992.

Asencio, Diego, and Nancy Asencio. *Our Man Inside*. New York: Little Brown and Company, 1983.

Aust, Stefan, *The Baader-Meinhof Group: The Inside Story of a Phenomenon*. Toronto: Random House/Canada, 1987.

Becker, Jillian. *Hitler's Children: The Story of the Baader-Meinhof Terrorist Gang*. Philadelphia: J.B. Lippincott Company, 1977.

Dobson, Christopher, and Ronald Payne. *The Carlos Complex: A Study in Terror*. London: Coronet Books, 1977.

———. *The Never-Ending War: Terrorism in the 80's*. New York: Facts on File, 1987.

Drake, Richard. *The Revolutionary Mystique and Terrorism in Contemporary Italy*. Bloomington, IN: Indiana University Press, 1989.

Farrell, William R. *Blood and Rage: The Story of the Japanese Red Army*. Lexington, MA: Lexington Books, 1990.

Kassimeris, George. *Europe's Last Red Terrorists: The Revolutionary Organization 17 November*. New York: New York University Press, 2001.

Koppel, Martin. *Peru's Shining Path: Anatomy of a Reactionary Sect*. New York: Pathfinder Press, 1984.

Laquer, Walter. *Terrorism*. London: Abacus Books, 1977.

MacDonald, Eileen. *Shoot the Women First*. New York: Random House, 1991.

Moxon-Browne, Edward. *European Terrorism*. New York: G. K. Hall & Co., 1994.

Palmer, David Scott. *The Shining Path of Peru*. New York: St. Martin's Press, 1994.

Rosie, George. *The Directory of International Terrorism*. Edinburgh, Scotland: Mainstream Books, 1986.

Sterling, Claire. *The Terror Network: The Secret War of International Terrorism*. New York: Berkley Books, 1981.

FURTHER READING AND WEBSITES

Books

Baer, Suzie. *Peru's MRTA: Tupac Amaru Revolutionary Movement*. NY: Rosen Publishing Group, 2003.

Behnke, Alison. *Italy in Pictures*. Minneapolis: Lerner Publications Company, 2003.

———. *Japan in Pictures*. Minneapolis: Lerner Publications Company, 2003.

Dower, John. *Embracing Defeat: Japan in the Wake of World War II*. New York: W. W. Norton & Company, 2000.

Gallagher, Aileen. *The Japanese Red Army*. NY: Rosen Publishing Group, 2003.

Hoffman, Bruce. *Inside Terrorism*. NY: Columbia University Press, 1998.

Kushner, Harvey W. *Encyclopedia of Terrorism*. Newbury Park, CA: Sage Publications, 2003.

Marquez, Heron. *Peru in Pictures*. Minneapolis: Lerner Publications Company, 2004.

Marx, Karl. *Selected Writings*. David McLennan, ed. Oxford: Oxford University Press, 2000.

Pipes, Richard. *Communism: A History*. New York: Modern Library, 2001.

Reich, Walter, ed. *Origins of Terrorism: Psychologies, Ideologies, Theologies, States of Mind*. Washington, D.C.: Woodrow Wilson Center Press, 1998.

Rius, Tom Englehardt, ed. *Marx for Beginners*. New York: David MacKay Co., 1990.

Sherman, Josephine. *The Cold War*. Minneapolis: Lerner Publications Company, 2004.

Stern, Steve J., ed. *Shining and Other Paths: War and Society in Peru, 1980–1995*. Durham, NC: Duke University Press, 1998.

Streissguth, Tom. *Colombia in Pictures*. Minneapolis: Lerner Publications Company, 2004.

Walker, Martin. *Cold War: A History*. New York: Henry Holt & Company, 1995.

Wilkinson, Paul. *Terrorism Versus Democracy: The Liberal State Response*. Cass Series on Political Violence, vol. 9. London: Frank Cass Publishers, 2000.

Zuehlke, Jeffrey. *Germany in Pictures*. Minneapolis: Lerner Publications Company, 2003.

Websites

BBC News World Edition
<http://news.bbc.co.uk/>
The website of the British Broadcasting Corporation provides extensive coverage of international news, as well as country profiles and in-depth reports on terrorist issues.

CNN.com
<http://www.cnn.com>
The Cable News Network site covers breaking news on terrorism and other world events. It also offers a searchable archive of past articles.

Economist.com
<http://www.economist.com>
Regularly updated, this online version of the *Economist* offers a news archive searchable by country and subject. It also offers commentary on how terrorist activities affect local economies and politics.

Terrorism
<http://www.teror.gen.tr/english>
This Turkish site examines terrorism in Europe, the Middle East, and other countries.

Terrorism: Questions and Answers
<http://terrorismanswers.com>
This site is operated by the Council on Foreign Relations and the Markle Foundation (a non-profit group that studies the media). It provides information on many terrorist groups and aspects of terrorism in a question-and-answer format.

The Terrorism Research Center
<http://www.homelandsecurity.com>
This comprehensive site offers profiles of terrorist groups, timelines of terrorist activities, counterterrorism information, and more.

Terrorist Group Profiles
<http://library.nps.navy.mil/home/tgp/tgp2.htm>
This website is run by the Dudley Knox Library at the U.S. Naval Postgraduate School in Monterey, California. It features profiles of terrorist groups, chronologies of terrorist incidents, and a link to the U.S. State Department.

This Is Baader-Meinhof
<http://www.baader-meinhof.com>
This website provides a timeline of Red Army Faction activities, a who's who, a guide to terminology, and more.

U.S. Department of State Counterterrorism Office
<http://www.state.gov/s/ct>
Maintained by the U.S. government, this site provides information on terrorist groups and their activities.

INDEX

ABOUT THE AUTHOR

Samuel M. Katz is an expert in the field of international terrorism and counterterrorism, military special operations, and law enforcement. He has written more than twenty books and dozens of articles on these subjects, as well as creating documentaries and giving lectures. Mr. Katz also serves as editor in chief of *Special Ops*, a magazine dedicated to the discussion of special operations around the world, and observes counterterrorism units in action in Europe and the Middle East. The Terrorist Dossiers series is his first foray into the field of juvenile nonfiction.

PHOTO ACKNOWLEDGMENTS

The photographs in this book appear courtesy of: © Hulton-Deutsch Collection/CORBIS, pp. 7, 24, 30; Library of Congress, LC_USZ62–116158, p. 9; © Bettman/CORBIS, pp. 10, 25; © Hulton Archive by Getty Images, pp. 11, 12, 14, 16, 21, 29, 33, 41, 42, 44; © Elio Ciol/ CORBIS, p. 17; © The Illustrated London News, p. 19; © AFP/CORBIS, pp. 27, 35, 49, 53, 58; © AP/Wide World Photos, pp. 34, 36; © National Archives, p. 39; © Reuters NewMedia Inc./CORBIS, pp. 45, 50, 52, 57; © Historical Society of Southern Florida, p. 48; Minneapolis Public Library, p. 56; © Daniel Lainé/CORBIS, p. 60; © Balaguer Alejandro/ CORBIS SYGMA, p. 61; © CORBIS SYGMA, p. 62. Front cover: © Balaguer Alejandro/ CORBIS SYGMA.